A Catholic Prayer Journal for Kids

Ask, and it will be given you; seek, and you will find; knock, and it will be opened to you.
– Matthew 7:7

Let the Children Come Unto Me by C. Vogelstein

A Catholic Prayer Journal

for kids

By Jennifer & Travis Rainey

createspace
an Amazon company

Seattle, Washington * Charleston, South Carolina

This book is dedicated to our sweet Joey.

This book is presented to

_____

on the occasion of

_____

_____

(Date)

Dear Parents,

Of all the lessons that we can give to our children, it is most important that we teach them to pray. Prayer is a conversation with God, and children should know from an early age that God is always there to listen to us and answer us. Saint John Paul II said, "Christian parents have the specific responsibility of educating their children in prayer, introducing them to gradual discovery of the mystery of God and to personal dialogue with Him."

If you have younger children, you will need to help them complete the prayers in this book. Older children might want to fill out this journal on their own. Either way, it is a good idea to read through the pages together so that you can discuss the different prayers and themes that are presented throughout the book. The journal has guided prayers, as well as blank pages where your children can write their own prayers.

The back of the journal has many different Catholic prayers, as well as pages where your child can list prayer requests and thanksgiving lists.

It is our prayer that this book will guide your children in a lifelong relationship with Our Lord and His Church.

Jennifer and Travis Rainey
April 2017

Guided Prayers

Sacred Heart by C.B. Chambers

Today I will pray...

for my walk with God.

In the name of the Father, and of the Son, and of the Holy Spirit. Amen.

Dear God,

Please help me to draw closer to you through my daily prayers. I also ask you to protect and guide my family, my friends, and myself. In particular, please help me with

_____

_____

_____

_____

Remember to start and end every prayer with "In the name of the Father, and of the Son, and of the Holy Spirit. Amen" while you make the Sign of the Cross.

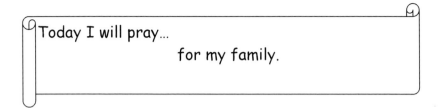

Today I will pray...

for my family.

Draw a picture of your family. As you draw each person, pray that God protects him or her.

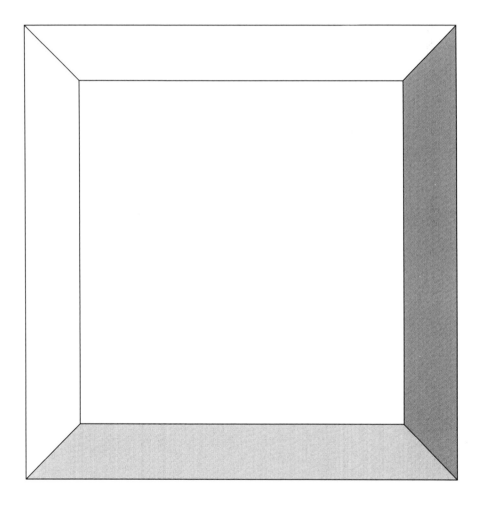

Today I will pray...

the Joyful Mysteries of the Most Holy Rosary.

The Joyful Mysteries are:
- **The Annunciation**: St. Gabriel tells Mary that God wants her to be Jesus' mother, and Mary says, "Yes."
- **The Visitation**: Mary visits her cousin Elizabeth who calls Mary "blessed among women."
- **The Nativity**: Jesus is born in Bethlehem.
- **The Presentation**: Mary and Joseph present Jesus in the Temple.
- **Finding Jesus in the Temple**: After Mary and Joseph search for Jesus for three days, they find Him in the Temple, His "Father's House."

Meditate on these Mysteries and pray one Hail Mary for each one.

When you "meditate" on the Rosary, you are thinking about each of these events in the lives of Jesus and Mary.

Today I will pray...

for my priest.

Dear Lord,

Thank you for my parish priest, Fr. _____. I ask that you care for him, guide him, and protect him. I am thankful for my priest because

_____

_____

_____

_____

_____

_____

You could send a card to your priest telling him how much you appreciate his work for God and for the parish.

Today I will pray...

in thanksgiving for the
gifts God has given me.

List several gifts that God has given to you. Tell Him how much you appreciate each one. Are you thankful for your family? Your friends? Nature? Your church?

_____

_____

_____

_____

Try to tell God something that you are thankful for each day.

Today I will pray...
                    the Our Father.

Our Father, Who art in Heaven,
Hallowed be Thy Name.
Thy Kingdom come.
Thy Will be done, on earth as it is in Heaven. Give us this
day our daily bread.
And forgive us our trespasses,
as we forgive those who trespass against us.
And lead us not into temptation,
but deliver us from evil. Amen.

God loves us, protects us, and provides for us. He is truly
our Father. Do I appreciate that God, the Creator of the
Universe, is my Father? How can I treat Him more like my
Father?

Today I will pray...

The Fatima Prayer.

Fill in the blanks. You can find this prayer on page 82.

O my Jesus, forgive us our _____, save us from the fires of hell, and lead all souls to _____, especially those most in _____ of Thy _____. Amen.

Our Lady of Fatima by C.B. Chambers

Our Blessed Mother gave this prayer to three shepherd children: Lucia, Jacinta, and Francisco, when she appeared at Fatima in 1917.

Today I will pray...

to the Blessed Virgin Mary.

When we pray to Mary, we are asking for her to intercede for us. It doesn't mean that we worship Mary. Only God (the Father, Son, and Holy Spirit) should be worshipped. Just like we would ask a friend to pray for us, we ask Mary to pray for us. Since she is Jesus' mother, she is a very powerful intercessor. Let's say a prayer to Mary.

Dear Mary,
I love you very much. Please ask Jesus to help me with

_____

_____

_____

_____

_____

An intercessor is someone who goes between two people asking for a favor. If your sister wanted a toy, but didn't want to ask your parents for it, you could be an intercessor by asking your parents for her. When we ask Mary and the saints to intercede for us, they are asking Jesus for a favor on our behalf.

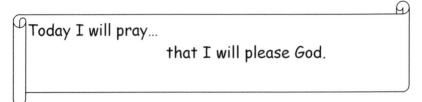

Today I will pray...

that I will please God.

Draw a picture that shows you doing something that would please God.

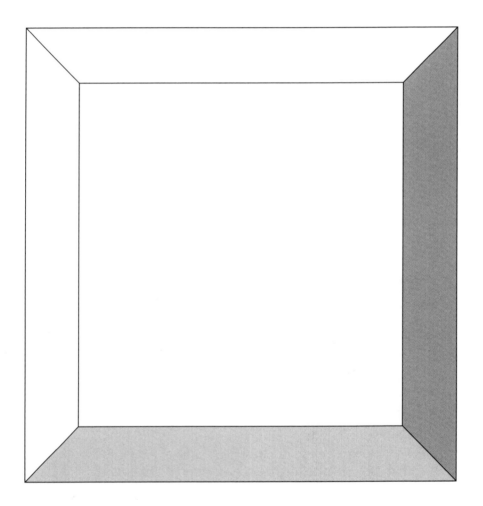

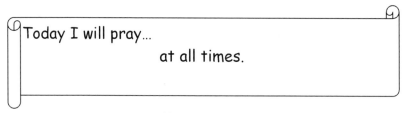

Today I will pray...

at all times.

"Pray at all times" (Ephesians 6:18).
"Pray constantly" (1 Thessalonians 5:17).

This might not seem possible, at least at first. When we "pray at all times," this should mean that we have God at the center of our lives and avoid sin throughout the day. It means that we think of God in the little things that we do. If you see a beautiful sunset, you say a short prayer of thanks. If you're worried about a test, you pray to remember the material. If you have done something wrong, you tell Jesus you're sorry. And you always try to think of God throughout the day.

How can I "pray constantly"?

_____

_____

_____

_____

_____

_____

_____

_____

Today I will pray...
                    at nighttime.

When I go to bed, I should tell God that I am thankful for the day that I have had. I should also ask him to protect and guide my family, my friends, and myself. And I should tell Him that I am sorry for what I did wrong during the day.

Dear God,

As I go to bed, I want to thank you for _____

_____

_____

_____

I want to ask you for _____

_____

_____

_____

I want to tell you I'm sorry for _____

_____

_____

_____

I love you. Amen.

Today I will pray...
                    the Hail Mary.

Hail Mary, Full of Grace, the Lord is with thee. Blessed art thou among women, and blessed is the fruit of thy womb, Jesus. Holy Mary, Mother of God, pray for us sinners now, and at the hour of our death. Amen.

Now copy the Hail Mary below:

_____

_____

_____

_____

_____

The Hail Mary prayer is based on Luke 1:28 and Luke 1:42.

Madonna of the Lilies by William-Adolphe Bouguereau

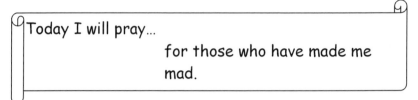

Today I will pray...

for those who have made me mad.

"But I say to you, Love your enemies and pray for those who persecute you" (Matthew 5:44).

Sometimes people make me angry. Sometimes my friends or family upset me or hurt my feelings, but I should remember to pray for them.

I always need to make sure that I let my parents or teachers know if someone hurts me, but I also need to pray for people who have made me mad. After all, every human is made in God's Image, and He loves us all.

I also need to remember that sometimes I am mean to people, too. We all do bad things from time to time, and when I do something wrong, I need to apologize to God and to the people who I have hurt.

Dear God, I want to pray for the people who have made me mad. I ask that you guide them, protect them, and that their actions are influenced by Your Love. I also ask

_____

_____

Today I will pray...

the Luminous Mysteries of the Most Holy Rosary.

The Luminous Mysteries are:
- **The Baptism in the Jordan:** St. John the Baptist baptizes Jesus.
- **The Wedding at Cana:** At Mary's request, Jesus turns water into wine.
- **The Proclamation of the Kingdom of God:** Jesus proclaims the Good News.
- **The Transfiguration:** Jesus shows His glory to His disciples.
- **The Institution of the Eucharist:** Jesus celebrates the first Mass at the Last Supper.

Meditate on these Mysteries and pray one Hail Mary for each one.

Breton Girl Praying Rosary
by A. Wagner

St. John Paul II added the Luminous Mysteries in 2002.

Today I will pray...
                   for the times when
                      I feel jealous.

Sometimes I feel jealous of other people. Maybe your friend just had a great birthday party, and you wish that you had the party instead. Maybe your brother got a new bike, and you want to take it from him.

It's not a good thing to be jealous. God doesn't want us to feel this way, but sometimes we feel jealous anyway. When we feel jealous, we should make a list of all of the things that we're thankful for. Also, we should try to feel happy for the person who has what we want. Think about it this way: you wouldn't want your friends to be mad at you because you had a new book or a new outfit. Most importantly, we should pray that we stop feeling this way.

Dear God,
Please help me when I'm jealous. I am so thankful for all that you have given me, like: _____

_____

_____

Please help me to not feel jealous of others, and please help me to be more thankful for all of the wonderful gifts that you have given to me. Amen.

Today I will pray...

for the Holy Father.

The Holy Father, or the Pope, is the leader of the Catholic Church on earth. We should pray for him every day, that he is protected, that he helps to spread God's message (the Gospel), and for his health and safety.

Dear God,
Please be with our Holy Father. I ask that

_____

_____

_____

_____

_____

_____

St. Peter was the first pope. There have been more than 265 popes since the Catholic Church started 2,000 years ago.

Today I will pray...
                    with the Psalms.

Look at a Bible, and find the book of Psalms. It is close to the middle of the Bible. Read Psalm 100.

Write in your own words what you think this Psalm means.

_____

_____

_____

The Song of the Angels
by William-Adolphe Bouguereau

We usually sing a Psalm in Mass on Sundays.

Today I will pray...
to St. Anthony and all of the saints.

Saint Anthony of Padua was a Franciscan priest who lived many centuries ago. He is now the saint who we can ask to help us find lost items. So, when you have lost a schoolbook or your favorite shirt, you can ask St. Anthony to help you find it.

Of course, we know that we can always pray straight to God, but it is also a wonderful idea to pray to the saints. The saints intercede for us, which means that they can ask God for us. The saints lived holy lives, and they are with God in Heaven, so they are happy to ask God to help us.

Dear St. Anthony,
I am so happy that you love God so much, and I want to be holy like you. Please ask God to help me become holy, too. Please help me when I have lost something. I also ask that

_____

_____

There are patron saints for most hobbies, jobs, countries, and much more! You can find lists online.

Today I will pray...

for someone who is sick.

Dear God,
Someone who I know is sick. Please help him (or her) to

_____

_____

_____

_____

_____

_____

_____

_____

Try to do something nice when someone is
sick. Make a card, bring flowers, or give
them a call to brighten their day.

Today I will pray...

for my family.

Dear God,

I love my family very much, and I want the best for each of them. Especially, I ask you

_____

_____

_____

_____

_____

_____

God gave us a wonderful gift when he gave us a family. Make sure that you thank Him every day for your family and all of your loved ones!

The Holy Family by Bayeu

Today I will pray...

for the times when I'm worried.

"Have no anxiety about anything, but in everything by prayer and supplication with thanksgiving let your requests be made known to God" (Philippians 4:6).

Dear God,

I know that you are always with me. When I am worried about something, please help me to trust in you.

When I am worried, I sometimes feel _____

_____

_____

_____

I sometimes worry about _____

_____

_____

_____

Please help me to see that you are with me. When I trust that you are always there for me, I feel _____

_____

_____

_____

Today I will pray...

the Glory Be.

Glory be to the Father, and to the Son,
and to the Holy Spirit.
As it was in the beginning, is now,
and ever shall be, world without end.

Amen.

You can copy the Glory Be on the lines below:

Thy Will Be Done by C.B. Chambers

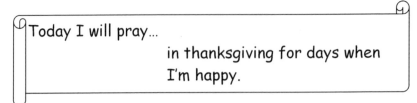

Today I will pray...

in thanksgiving for days when I'm happy.

Draw a picture of something that makes you happy. Then tell God how thankful you are.

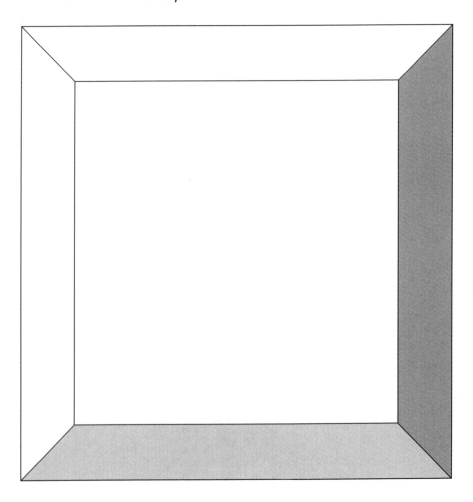

Today I will pray...

the Morning Offering.

This is the Morning Offering that adults say:

O Jesus, through the Immaculate Heart of Mary, I offer
You my prayers, works, joys and sufferings of this day for
all the intentions of Your Sacred Heart, in union with the
Holy Sacrifice of the Mass throughout the world,
in reparation for my sins, for the intentions of all my
relatives and friends, and in particular for the intentions
of the Holy Father. Amen.

You could pray that version, or you could pray your own. In
the morning offering, you should offer your whole day to
God, including all of your work, your playtime, your joys,
and sadness. You can write your own version here:

Today I will pray...

when I am misunderstood.

Sometimes, people don't understand me. Maybe I said something that accidentally hurt someone's feelings, or I accidentally made someone mad. I feel bad that this happened, but I know that it happens to everyone from time to time.

Dear God,
Please help me when I have bee n misunderstood. I ask that you

_____

_____

_____

_____

Help me to apologize if this has hurt my friend or family member. Help me to tell them

_____

_____

_____

_____

When this happens, try to explain it to the person who didn't understand you.

Today I will pray...
                    the Memorare.

Memorare

Remember, O most gracious Virgin Mary, that never was it known that anyone who fled to thy protection, implored thy help, or sought thine intercession was left unaided.

Inspired by this confidence, I fly unto thee, O Virgin of virgins, my mother; to thee do I come, before thee I stand, sinful and sorrowful. O Mother of the Word Incarnate, despise not my petitions, but in thy mercy hear and answer me. Amen.

What does this prayer mean to you? Could you write one or two sentences that summarize this prayer?

_____

_____

_____

_____

_____

The Memorare prayer is 600 years old.

Today I will pray...

the Guardian Angel Prayer.

Angel of God, my guardian dear,
To whom God's love commits me here,
Ever this day, be at my side,
To light and guard, Rule and guide. Amen.

Now, copy this prayer on the lines below.

_____

_____

_____

_____

Guardian Angel by Kaulbach

Today I will pray...

for the times when I have
disobeyed.

Dear God,
Sometimes I disobey my parents or my teachers. I know
that this is wrong, and I'm sorry. Please help me to

_____

_____

_____

Help me to tell them that I am sorry. Sometimes that can
be difficult, but I know that I should do it. Also, help me
to be more obedient in the future. It's hard for me to obey
sometimes because _____

_____

_____

_____

I also know that I should be obedient to you, dear Lord.
Here are the ways that I will obey your rules:

- _____

- _____

- _____

- _____

Today I will pray...

in thanksgiving for all of the people who love me.

It is such a gift to love people and for them to love you in return. List several people who love you. Tell God that you are thankful for each one, and ask that God will pour His blessings on them.

- _____

- _____

- _____

- _____

- _____

- _____

Today I will pray...

grace before and after meals.

Grace Before Meals
Bless us, O Lord, and these Thy gifts, which we are about to receive from Thy bounty, through Christ our Lord. Amen.

Grace After Meals
We give Thee thanks for all your benefits, O Almighty God, Who lives and reigns forever; and may the souls of the faithful departed, through the mercy of God, rest in peace. Amen.

Write your own prayer thanking God for your food:

Dear God,

_____

_____

_____

Try to remember to pray the Grace Before Meals and Grace After Meals today.

Today I will pray...
                    when I'm having a bad day.

Dear God,
Some days are difficult. Maybe I am sick, or someone was mean to me. Maybe I was hurt, or maybe I got in trouble. Even though I am upset right now, I know that you are with me. You are always there with me.

Dear God,
Please remind me that you are with me when I'm having a bad day. Help me to _____

_____

_____

_____

_____

When you're upset, you can "offer up" your suffering for other people. This means that you are asking God that your problems, sadness, and pains will help someone else. It's always best to focus on others, even when you are sad.

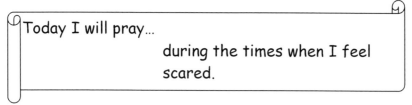

Today I will pray...

> during the times when I feel scared.

"Pray, hope and don't worry." - St. Padre Pio

Draw a picture of something that scares you. Then draw your Guardian Angel protecting you.

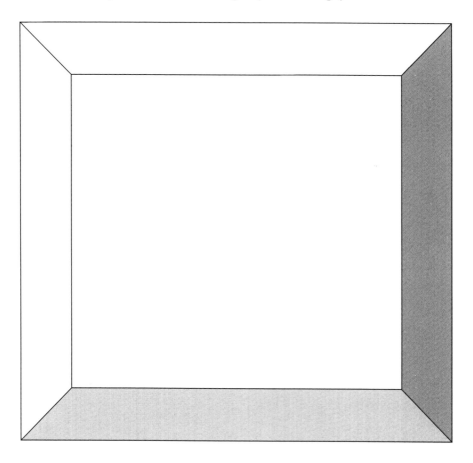

Today I will pray...

in thanksgiving for my teachers.

Dear God,
I am very thankful for my teachers. They work so hard to teach me. I am thankful for them because

- _____

- _____

- _____

- _____

And I ask that you protect them, guide them, and inspire them through their very special job. Amen.

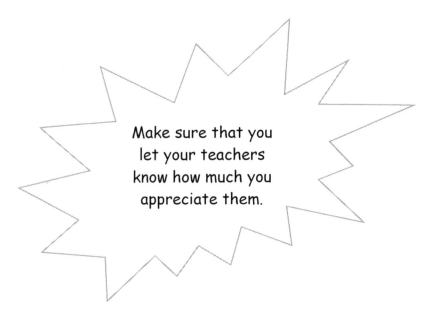

Make sure that you let your teachers know how much you appreciate them.

Today I will pray...

for the times when I am mad.

Dear God,

Sometimes I get mad. I get mad when _____

_____

I know that everyone feels mad sometimes, but it's not a good feeling. Please help me to understand that I sometimes make people mad, too. I make people mad by

_____

_____

Please help me to be mad less often. When I'm mad, remind me to forgive the people who upset me. Amen.

Remember to pray for the people who make you mad.

Meditation
by William-Adolphe Bouguereau

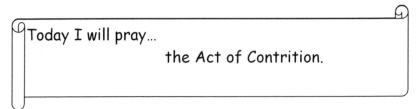

Today I will pray...

the Act of Contrition.

Here is the Act of Contrition that adults (and some children) say:

O my God, I am heartily sorry for having offended Thee, and I detest all my sins, because I dread the loss of Heaven and the pains of Hell; but most of all because they offend Thee, my God, Who art all good and deserving of all my love. I firmly resolve, with the help of Thy grace, to confess my sins, to do penance and to amend my life. Amen.

Write your own prayer asking God to forgive you when you sin:

Dear God,

_____

_____

_____

_____

_____

_____

_____

_____

_____

_____

Today I will pray...

that I will do God's Will.

"I can't do big things, but I want everything to be for the glory of God." - St. Dominic Savio

Dear God,
I know that I am still young, but I know that I can work for you. I can be a witness to others by showing your love to them. I can help others, and I can pray. Maybe I can't drive a car or have a job, but I can do something much more important: I can be a strong Christian. Please help me to become more like you. Please help me in the areas where I can become a better person, such as _____

_____

I want to be a saint because _____

_____

Jesus & the Small Child by Carl Bloch

Today I will pray...

for God's Will to be done.

Sometimes we don't know exactly how we should pray, but God always knows what is best for us. If we say that we pray for God's Will, then we are uniting our will to God's Will. In other words, when we pray for God's Will to be done, we are telling God that we trust Him to show us the right direction that we should take.

In your own words, why should we pray for God's Will?

_____

_____

_____

_____

_____

"The prayer of a righteous man has great power in its effects" (James 5:16). We are righteous when we follow God's laws, and our prayers are especially powerful when we avoid sin.

Today I will pray...

that I show love to my family.

Dear God,
I love my family very much. Please show me how to love them even more. Amen.

Here are a few ways that I can show love to my family:

- _____
- _____
- _____
- _____
- _____

"Spread love everywhere you go: first of all in your own house... Let no one ever come to you without leaving better and happier. Be the living expression of God's kindness; kindness in your face, kindness in your eyes, kindness in your smile, kindness in your warm greeting."
- Saint Mother Teresa of Calcutta

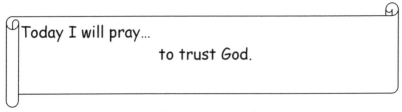

Today I will pray...
to trust God.

"Fear not because God is with you."
- St. Padre Pio

Dear God,
Sometimes I am scared, but I know that you are always with me. Maybe I can't see you, but you are always (always!) by my side. I can ask you to protect me when I feel scared. I feel scared when _____

_____

_____

When I am scared, please _____

_____

_____

_____

_____

"When I am afraid, I put my
trust in thee."
- Psalm 56:3

Today I will pray...

the Sorrowful Mysteries of the Most Holy Rosary.

The Sorrowful Mysteries are:
- **The Agony in the Garden:** Jesus prays in the Garden of Gethsemane.
- **The Scourging at the Pillar:** Jesus is whipped.
- **The Crowning with Thorns**
- **The Carrying of the Cross**
- **The Crucifixion**

Meditate on these Mysteries and pray one Hail Mary for each one.

Agony in the Garden by Gustave Dore

Today I will pray...

for our Church family.

Draw a picture of some of the people who go to your parish. Don't forget your priest! Then pray for these people.

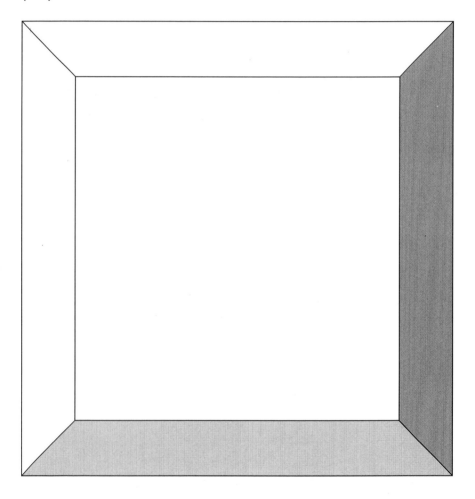

Today I will pray...

in thanksgiving for my family.

I love my family very much. Here are the reasons that I am thankful for them:

- _____

- _____

- _____

- _____

- _____

- _____

- _____

The Glorious Mysteries are:
- **The Resurrection:** Jesus rises from the dead.
- **The Ascension:** Jesus ascends into Heaven.
- **The Descent of the Holy Spirit:** The Holy Spirit descends onto the disciples.
- **The Assumption:** The Blessed Mother is brought into Heaven.
- **The Coronation of the Blessed Virgin Mary:** Mary is crowned Queen of Heaven.

Meditate on these Mysteries and pray one Hail Mary for each one.

Resurrection by Carl Bloch

Today I will pray...
the Divine Praises.

Fill in the blanks. You can find this prayer on page 83.

The Divine Praises

Blessed be God. Blessed be his Holy _____.

Blessed be Jesus Christ, true God and true _____.

Blessed be the Name of Jesus.

Blessed be his most _____ _____.

Blessed be his _____ Precious Blood.

Blessed be Jesus in the most Holy Sacrament of the Altar.

Blessed be the Holy Spirit, the _____.

Blessed be the great Mother of God, Mary most holy.

Blessed be her _____ and Immaculate Conception.

Blessed be her glorious _____.

Blessed be the name of Mary, Virgin and _____.

Blessed be St. _____, her most chaste spouse.

Blessed be God in his _____ and in his saints.

Today I will pray...

in thanksgiving for the wonders that God made.

List the reasons you are thankful for nature.

- _____

- _____

- _____

- _____

"The heavens are telling the glory of God; and the firmament proclaims his handiwork."
- Psalm 19:1

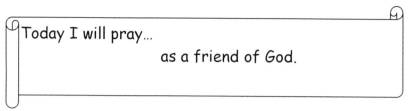

Today I will pray...

as a friend of God.

"For prayer is nothing else than being on terms of friendship with God." – St. Teresa of Avila

Do I consider God to be my friend? Do I enjoy spending time with Him in prayer? How can I tell Him that He is my friend?

My Own Prayers

Immaculate Heart by C.B. Chambers

Today I will pray for...

_____

In the name of the Father, and of the Son, and of the Holy Spirit. Amen.
Dear God,

_____

_____

_____

_____

_____

_____

Today I will pray for...

_____

In the name of the Father, and of the Son, and of
the Holy Spirit. Amen.
Dear God,

_____

_____

_____

_____

_____

_____

Today I will pray for...

_____

In the name of the Father, and of the Son, and of the Holy Spirit. Amen.
Dear God,

_____

_____

_____

_____

_____

_____

Today I will pray for…

_____

In the name of the Father, and of the Son, and of the Holy Spirit. Amen.
Dear God,

_____

_____

_____

_____

_____

_____

Today I will pray for...

_____

In the name of the Father, and of the Son, and of
the Holy Spirit. Amen.
Dear God,

_____

_____

_____

_____

_____

_____

Today I will pray for...

_____

In the name of the Father, and of the Son, and of the Holy Spirit. Amen.
Dear God,

_____

_____

_____

_____

_____

_____

Today I will pray for...

_____

In the name of the Father, and of the Son, and of the Holy Spirit. Amen.
Dear God,

_____

_____

_____

_____

_____

_____

Today I will pray for...

_____

In the name of the Father, and of the Son, and of the Holy Spirit. Amen.
Dear God,

_____

_____

_____

_____

_____

_____

Today I will pray for...

_____

In the name of the Father, and of the Son, and of the Holy Spirit. Amen.
Dear God,

_____

_____

_____

_____

_____

_____

Today I will pray for...

_____

In the name of the Father, and of the Son, and of
the Holy Spirit. Amen.
Dear God,

_____

_____

_____

_____

_____

_____

Today I will pray for...

_____

In the name of the Father, and of the Son, and of the Holy Spirit. Amen.
Dear God,

_____

_____

_____

_____

_____

_____

_____

Today I will pray for...

_____

In the name of the Father, and of the Son, and of the Holy Spirit. Amen.
Dear God,

_____

_____

_____

_____

_____

_____

Today I will pray for...

_____

In the name of the Father, and of the Son, and of
the Holy Spirit. Amen.
Dear God,

_____

_____

_____

_____

_____

_____

Today I will pray for...

_____

In the name of the Father, and of the Son, and of the Holy Spirit. Amen.

Dear God,

_____

_____

_____

_____

_____

_____

Today I will pray for...

_____

In the name of the Father, and of the Son, and of the Holy Spirit. Amen.
Dear God,

_____

_____

_____

_____

_____

_____

Today I will pray for...

_____

In the name of the Father, and of the Son, and of
the Holy Spirit. Amen.
Dear God,

_____

_____

_____

_____

_____

_____

Today I will pray for...

_____

In the name of the Father, and of the Son, and of the Holy Spirit. Amen.
Dear God,

_____

_____

_____

_____

_____

_____

Today I will pray for...

_____

In the name of the Father, and of the Son, and of the Holy Spirit. Amen.

Dear God,

_____

_____

_____

_____

_____

_____

Today I will pray for...

_____

In the name of the Father, and of the Son, and of the Holy Spirit. Amen.
Dear God,

_____

_____

_____

_____

_____

_____

Today I will pray for…

_____

In the name of the Father, and of the Son, and of
the Holy Spirit. Amen.
Dear God,

_____

_____

_____

_____

_____

_____

_____

Today I will pray for...

_____

In the name of the Father, and of the Son, and of
the Holy Spirit. Amen.
Dear God,

_____

_____

_____

_____

_____

_____

Today I will pray for...

_____

In the name of the Father, and of the Son, and of the Holy Spirit. Amen.
Dear God,

_____

_____

_____

_____

_____

_____

Today I will pray for...

_____

In the name of the Father, and of the Son, and of the Holy Spirit. Amen.
Dear God,

_____

_____

_____

_____

_____

_____

Today I will pray for…

_____

In the name of the Father, and of the Son, and of the Holy Spirit. Amen.
Dear God,

_____

_____

_____

_____

_____

_____

_____

Catholic Prayers

The Prayer by William-Adolphe Bouguereau

The Our Father

Our Father who art in Heaven, hallowed be Thy name; Thy Kingdom come; Thy will be done on earth as it is in Heaven. Give us this day our daily bread; and forgive us our trespasses as we forgive those who trespass against us; and lead us not into temptation, but deliver us from evil. Amen.

The Hail Mary

Hail Mary, full of grace! The Lord is with thee; blessed art thou among women, and blessed is the fruit of thy womb, Jesus. Holy Mary, Mother of God, pray for us sinners, now and at the hour of our death. Amen.

The Glory Be

Glory be to the Father, and to the Son, and to the Holy Spirit. As it was in the beginning, is now, and ever shall be, world without end. Amen.

The Fatima Prayer

O my Jesus, forgive us our sins, save us from the fires of hell, and lead all souls to Heaven, especially those most in need of Thy mercy. Amen.

Grace Before Meals

Bless us, O Lord, and these Thy gifts, which we are about to receive from Thy bounty, through Christ our Lord. Amen.

Grace After Meals

We give Thee thanks for all your benefits, O Almighty God, Who lives and reigns forever; and may the souls of the faithful departed, through the mercy of God, rest in peace. Amen.

Hail, Holy Queen

Hail, holy Queen, mother of mercy, our life, our sweetness, and our hope. To thee do we cry, poor banished children of Eve. To thee do we send up our sighs mourning and weeping in this valley of tears. Turn then, most gracious advocate, thine eyes of mercy toward us, and after this our exile show us the blessed fruit of thy womb, Jesus.

O clement, O loving, O sweet Virgin Mary.

Pray for us, O Holy Mother of God.

That we may be made worthy of the promises of Christ.

The Divine Praises

Blessed be God.
Blessed be his Holy Name.
Blessed be Jesus Christ, true God and true Man.
Blessed be the Name of Jesus.
Blessed be his most Sacred Heart.
Blessed be his most Precious Blood.
Blessed be Jesus in the most Holy Sacrament of the Altar.
Blessed be the Holy Spirit, the Paraclete.
Blessed be the great Mother of God, Mary most holy.
Blessed be her holy and Immaculate Conception.
Blessed be her glorious Assumption.
Blessed be the name of Mary, Virgin and Mother.
Blessed be St. Joseph, her most chaste spouse.
Blessed be God in his angels and in his saints.

The Morning Offering

O Jesus, through the Immaculate Heart of Mary, I offer You my prayers, works, joys and sufferings of this day for all the intentions of Your Sacred Heart, in union with the Holy Sacrifice of the Mass throughout the world, in reparation for my sins, for the intentions of all my relatives and friends, and in particular for the intentions of the Holy Father. Amen.

Memorare

Remember, O most gracious Virgin Mary, that never was it known that anyone who fled to thy protection, implored thy help, or sought thine intercession was left unaided.

Inspired by this confidence, I fly unto thee, O Virgin of virgins, my mother; to thee do I come, before thee I stand, sinful and sorrowful. O Mother of the Word Incarnate, despise not my petitions, but in thy mercy hear and answer me. Amen.

The Act of Contrition

O my God, I am heartily sorry for having offended Thee, and I detest all my sins, because I dread the loss of Heaven and the pains of Hell; but most of all because they offend Thee, my God, Who art all good and deserving of all my love. I firmly resolve, with the help of Thy grace, to confess my sins, to do penance and to amend my life. Amen.

Prayer to Saint Michael the Archangel

Saint Michael the Archangel, defend us in battle. Be our defense against the wickedness and snares of the Devil. May God rebuke him, we humbly pray, and do thou, O Prince of the Heavenly hosts, by the power of God, thrust into hell Satan, and all the evil spirits, who prowl about the world seeking the ruin of souls. Amen.

The Creed

I believe in God, the Father almighty, Creator of Heaven and earth, and in Jesus Christ, His only Son, our Lord. He was conceived by the Holy Spirit, and born of the Virgin Mary. He suffered under Pontius Pilate, was crucified, died and was buried. He descended into hell. On the third day He rose again. He ascended into Heaven, and is seated at the right hand of God the Father Almighty. He will come again to judge the living and the dead.

I believe in the Holy Spirit, the Holy Catholic Church, the communion of saints, the forgiveness of sins, the resurrection of the body, and life everlasting. Amen.

The Guardian Angel Prayer

Angel of God, my guardian dear, to whom God's love commits me here, ever this day be at my side to light and guard, to rule and guide. Amen.

The Holy Rosary

1. Make the Sign of the Cross and say "In the name of the Father, and of the Son, and of the Holy Spirit. Amen."

2. Say the Creed (page 85).

3. Say one Our Father, three Hail Marys, and one Glory Be (page 82).

4. Announce the first Mystery (look on the next page for the Mysteries). Then pray one Our Father, ten Hail Marys, one Glory Be, and one Fatima Prayer. (page 82)

5. Then pray one Our Father, ten Hail Marys, one Glory Be, and one Fatima Prayer for each Mystery.

6. After you have completed all the decades, say the Hail, Holy Queen (page 83).

7. Make the Sign of the Cross and say, "In the Name of the Father, and of the Son, and of the Holy Spirit. Amen."

The Mysteries of the Rosary

The Joyful Mysteries
(Mondays and Saturdays, and Sundays during Advent and Christmas):

1. The Annunciation
2. The Visitation
3. The Nativity
4. The Presentation
5. The Finding of Jesus in the Temple

The Sorrowful Mysteries
(Tuesdays and Fridays, and Sundays during Lent):

1. Agony in the Garden
2. Scourging at the Pillar
3. Crowning with Thorns
4. Carrying of the Cross
5. The Crucifixion

The Glorious Mysteries
(Wednesdays and Sundays):

1. The Resurrection
2. The Ascension
3. The Descent of the Holy Spirit
4. The Assumption of the Blessed Virgin Mary
5. The Coronation of the Blessed Virgin Mary

The Luminous Mysteries
(Thursdays):

1. Baptism in the Jordan
2. The Wedding at Cana
3. Proclamation of the Kingdom
4. The Transfiguration
5. Institution of the Eucharist

The Divine Mercy Chaplet

Step 1 – Using a Rosary, begin at the cross by making the Sign of the Cross.

(Optional Opening Prayer)
You expired, Jesus, but the source of life gushed forth for souls, and the ocean of mercy opened up for the whole world. O Fount of Life, unfathomable Divine Mercy, envelop the whole world and empty Yourself out upon us.

Step 2 - O Blood and Water, which gushed forth from the Heart of Jesus as a fountain of Mercy for us, I trust in You! (Repeat three times)

Step 3 – On the three beads of the Rosary pray the Our Father, the Hail Mary and the Apostles' Creed.

Step 4 – Begin each decade with the Our Father beads by praying this prayer:

Eternal Father, I offer You the Body and Blood, Soul and Divinity of Your dearly beloved Son, Our Lord Jesus Christ, in atonement for our sins and those of the whole world.

Step 5 – Complete the decade on the 10 Hail Mary beads by praying this prayer:

For the sake of His Sorrowful Passion, have mercy on us and on the whole world.

Repeat steps 4 and 5 for each decade.

Step 6 – After praying all five decades, pray the following prayer 3 times:

Holy God, Holy Mighty One, Holy Immortal One, have mercy on us and on the whole world.

Step 7 – (Optional Closing Prayer)
Eternal God, in whom mercy is endless and the treasury of compassion inexhaustible, look kindly upon us, and increase Your mercy in us, that in difficult moments, we might not despair nor become despondent, but with great confidence, submit ourselves to Your holy will, which is Love and Mercy itself.

Amen.

Scripture Verses
To Memorize

For God so loved the world that he gave his only Son, that whoever believes in him should not perish but have eternal life.
– John 3:16

We know that in everything God works for good with those who love him, who are called according to his purpose.
– Romans 8:28

If God is for us, who is against us?
– Romans 8:31

Do not be anxious about your life, what you shall eat or what you shall drink, nor about your body, what you shall put on. Is not life more than food, and the body more than clothing?
– Matthew 6:25

I can do all things in him who strengthens me.
– Philippians 4:13

They who wait for the LORD shall renew their strength, they shall mount up with wings like eagles, they shall run and not be weary, they shall walk and not faint.
- Isaiah 40:31

My Favorite Bible Verses

_____

_____

_____

_____

_____

_____

_____

_____

_____

Prayer Intentions

_____

_____

_____

_____

_____

_____

_____

_____

_____

Prayer Intentions

_____

_____

_____

_____

_____

_____

_____

_____

I am thankful for...

_____

_____

_____

_____

_____

_____

_____

_____

_____

I am thankful for...

_____

_____

_____

_____

_____

_____

_____

_____

_____

_____

I am thankful for...

_____

_____

_____

_____

_____

_____

_____

_____

_____

I am thankful for...

_____

_____

_____

_____

_____

_____

_____

_____

_____

Notes

Notes

Made in the USA
San Bernardino, CA
19 April 2018